It's me... a Giraffe

Om KIDZ
An imprint of Om Books International

First Published in 2019 by

Om Kidz | Om Books International

Corporate & Editorial Office
A-12, Sector 64, Noida 201 301
Uttar Pradesh, India
Phone: +91 120 477 4100
Email: editorial@ombooks.com
Website: www.ombooksinternational.com

Sales Office
107, Ansari Road, Darya Ganj
New Delhi 110 002, India
Phone: +91 11 4000 9000
Email: sales@ombooks.com
Website: www.ombooks.com

ISBN: 978-93-86410-48-1

Printed in India

10 9 8 7 6 5 4 3 2 1

Contents

WHO ARE YOU?

Hello! I am a giraffe. I have a long neck, which is one of my most unique characteristics.

Scientific Name

Giraffa

HOW TALL ARE YOU?

We are the tallest land animals. Male giraffes are around 5.5 m tall and weigh up to 1930 kg. Female giraffes are almost 4.5 m tall and weigh around 1180 kg.

Cows and Bulls

While male giraffes are known as bulls, female giraffes are called cows.

WHAT ARE YOUR BABIES CALLED?

Baby giraffes are called calves. A baby giraffe is around 2 m tall and weighs around 100 kg.

HOW DO YOU TAKE CARE OF YOUR CALVES?

The mother giraffe licks and nuzzles her calf for almost a week after its birth. During this time they become familiar with each other's scent.

Later, the calf is left with a 'nursery group' of calves, while mother giraffes **forage** in the nearby areas.

A new word to learn

Forage - search for food

WHEN DO THE CALVES START EATING?

The calves start munching on vegetation when they are around three weeks old. They continue suckling for 18 to 22 months.

Up and About

Most calves can stand up and walk within an hour of their birth.

HOW DO YOU COMMUNICATE?

We snort, grunt and hum to communicate with each other. Mother giraffes often nuzzle and stroke their calves to show affection.

Humming to Ourselves

We make humming sounds during the night. Humans may not be able to hear us humming because we make very low-frequency sounds.

WHERE DO YOU LIVE?

We are commonly found in the grasslands and the open woodlands of East Africa. You can also come and see us at wildlife sanctuaries, such as the Serengeti National Park in Tanzania and the Amboseli National Park in Kenya.

DO YOU LIVE ALONE?

No, we live in groups. There can be up to 20 giraffes in one group. We are non-territorial, social animals.

Lifespan

Giraffes can live for almost 26 years in the wild. They live slightly longer in captivity.

DO YOU HAVE HORNS?

Yes. Both male and female giraffes have a pair of horns each. Male giraffes also have other bony bulges on their head.

Excellent Eyesight

Giraffes have excellent eyesight. This helps them keep track of their herd over long distances.

WHAT IS THE COLOUR OF YOUR TONGUE?

Our tongues are dark blue, black or purple. They are over half-a-metre long. The dark colour of our tongue is known to protect it from sunburn.

WHAT DO YOU EAT?

We like eating new leaves and shoots. We enjoy munching on the leaves of thorny acacia trees. Female giraffes like feeding on high-energy low-fibre food.

Antiseptic Saliva

A giraffe's saliva has antiseptic properties. If its tongue gets injured while eating thorny leaves, its saliva heals the wounds.

DO YOU HAVE TEETH?

Yes, we have 32 teeth. Also, our tongue and the inside of our mouths are coated with tough tissues for protection. We grasp the leaves with our lips or tongue and pull them into our mouth.

Massive Appetite

Giraffes have huge appetites. A large male giraffe can eat up to 65 kg of food in a day.

HOW OFTEN DO YOU DRINK WATER?

Most of our water requirements are fulfilled through the food we eat. However, during the dry season we drink water at least every three days to **quench** our thirst.

CAN YOU SIT?

Yes, we can! However, we spend most of our lives standing. We even sleep and give birth standing.

A new word to learn

Quench - satisfying thirst

Standing Tall

Giraffes are so tall that they have to spread their forelegs apart in order to bend their head and reach the ground.

HOW LONG IS YOUR NECK?

My neck is around 1.8 m long. It has only seven **vertebrae**. I have several large muscles which support my head and neck.

A new word to learn

Vertebrae - series of small bones forming the backbone

DO YOU SLEEP?

Of course we do. However, unlike humans, we need very little sleep! We take quick naps that may last not more than one or two minutes.

WHO ALL ARE THERE IN YOUR FAMILY?

My family includes the northern giraffe, the southern giraffe, the reticulated giraffe and the Masai giraffe.

Northern Giraffes

They are also known as the three-horned giraffes. They are native to North Africa.

Southern Giraffes

They have reddish-brown irregular patches on their body. They are mainly found in South Africa.

Reticulated Giraffes

They are also known as the Somali giraffes. The blocks on their body sometimes appear deep red and even cover their legs. They are the most commonly seen giraffes in zoos.

Masai Giraffes

They are also known as the Kilimanjaro giraffes. These giraffes are native to East Africa and Kenya. The jagged, star-like blotched patterns on their coat reach down to their hooves.

Activity Time

Giraffe Finger Puppet

Things You'll Need

- Yellow, brown and pink cardstock paper
- 0.75-inch circle punch
- Scissors
- Glue bottle
- Brown wool
- Googly eyes
- Marker

Using the yellow cardstock paper, cut out a 2.5-inch circle, a 3.5-inch circle, two small ears and a rectangular-shaped giraffe neck. Also, use pink and brown cardstock paper to cut out a shout and horns for the giraffe puppet.

Punch out two 0.75-inch circles at the bottom of the larger circle, to make holes for the finger puppet. Glue the giraffe's neck and head onto the larger circle.

Paste the snout, horns, ears and googly eyes on the face of the giraffe.

Using a marker draw the nose and mouth. Cut four short lengths of brown wool and paste them over the giraffe's head. Cut the brown cardstock paper into tiny bits and paste these on the giraffe's body. Wait for the glue to dry.

Your giraffe finger puppet is now ready. Enjoy!

The giraffe is hungry! Help it reach the tree, so that it can munch on the yummy leaves.